The Marriage of Aphrodite and Hephaestus

Mythology and Folklore
Children's Greek & Roman Books

Speedy Publishing LLC

40 E. Main St. #1156

Newark, DE 19711

www.speedypublishing.com

Copyright 2017

In this book, we're going to talk about the marriage of Aphrodite and Hephaestus. So, let's get right to it!

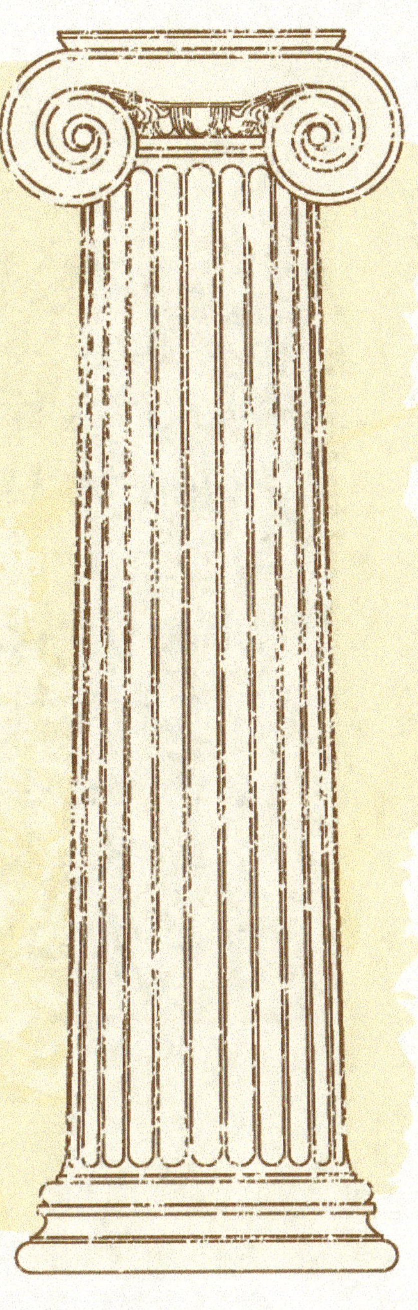

The ancient Greeks worshipped many different gods and goddesses. Their gods and goddesses often had superhuman powers and were immortal, but they weren't perfect. In fact, they had strengths and weaknesses in their personalities just like humans did. There were twelve gods and goddesses who were more important than the others and they lived on Mount Olympus. Both Aphrodite and Hephaestus were among these twelve.

APHRODITE

WHO WAS APHRODITE?

Aphrodite was a beautiful goddess who emerged full grown from the sea foam off the Greek island called Cyprus. This story about her birth comes from the Greek author and poet Hesiod. His book, Theogony, describes the history of the gods and goddesses. However, there are other stories about Aphrodite's birth as well.

According to the Iliad, authored by Homer, Aphrodite was the daughter of the god of gods, Zeus, and an ancient goddess by the name of Dione. Aphrodite is known as Venus in Roman mythology and she is the goddess of beauty, love, pleasure, and fertility.

ZEUS

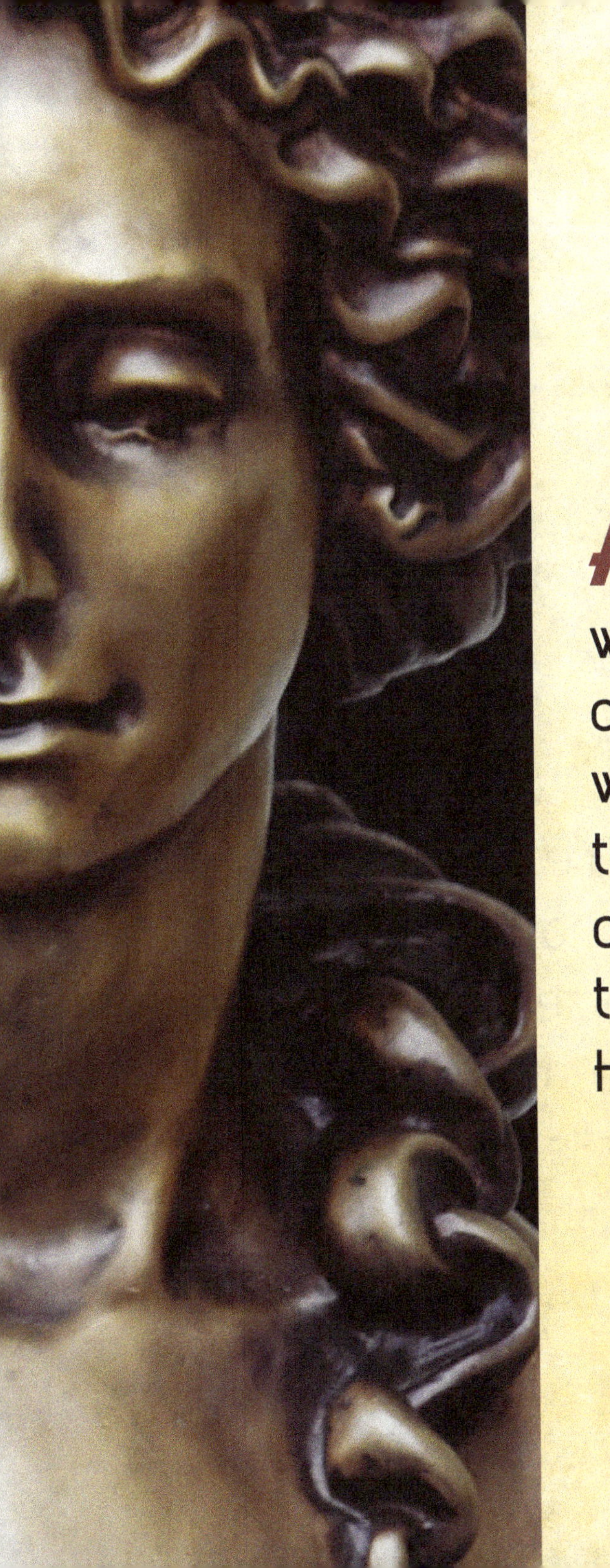

Aphrodite was so beautiful that some of the gods were worried that she would create rivalry and possibly a war among them. To solve this potential problem, Zeus decided to marry her off to the ugly, crippled god Hephaestus.

WHO WAS HEPHAESTUS?

Hephaestus was essentially the blacksmith for the gods. He worked with fire and metalworking and in Roman mythology his name is Vulcan. The words "volcano" and "vulcanize," which are both words related to fire, can be traced back to his name. In Theogony, Hesiod tells that the goddess Hera, Zeus's main wife, gave birth to Hephaestus by herself, without a god or man as the baby's father.

HEPHAESTUS

HERA

Hera was always angry with Zeus because he wasn't faithful to her. It's possible that she gave birth to Hephaestus in this way to get revenge on Zeus, who had brought forth the goddess Athena without Hera.

ANCIENT GREEK GODS AND DEITIES

The twelve gods and goddesses of Mount Olympus were known for their beauty and athletic prowess. However, Hera's baby Hephaestus was rather ugly and some stories said he was crippled or had a limp. The shallow Hera couldn't accept this deformed child as her own, so she cast him off the mountain.

CLIFFS NEAR FANARAKI ON LEMNOS ISLAND

After a very long fall, he fell into the waters near Lemnos, a Greek island. Fortunately for Hephaestus, two water deities saved him, but he grew up not knowing anything about his birth.

ΗΦΑΙΣΤΟΥ

Another story about Hephaestus says that he was the offspring of Zeus and Hera and that he was older when Zeus threw him off of Mount Olympus. There are several theories as to why Zeus was so angry that he threw his son off the mountain, crippling him.

One of the theories is that Hephaestus was trying to shield his mother from Zeus's anger. At one point, Zeus had bound his wife with chains of gold and she was suspended midair between the heavens and the Earth.

It was Zeus's revenge for when she had had him placed into a deep, hypnotic sleep so that she could go after Zeus's son Heracles, more commonly known as Hercules. Hera hated Hercules because Zeus had fathered him with a mortal woman.

HEAD OF HERACLES

In any case, Hephaestus was nurtured by the tribe living on the island called Sintians, who were ancient Greek pirates. He grew up there and learned to make beautiful, elaborate pieces of jewelry for the water deities who had saved him.

HEPHAESTUS HAS HIS REVENGE

The gods and goddesses always seemed to be seeking revenge on one another. Hephaestus sought revenge on his mother for either rejecting him by throwing him off Mount Olympus or not protecting him when Zeus threw him off. To get his revenge, Hephaestus created an amazing throne made of gold and had it sent to Mount Olympus for Hera.

Hera thought this regal chair was fit only for her, but as soon as she sat in it, it surrounded her and she wasn't able to get up. Hera wasn't well liked and the other gods and goddesses could have left her there, but her powers were needed at that time so something had to be done.

When Hephaestus refused to release his evil mother, the only god who could persuade him to extract her was Dionysus. She did this not through reason, but by getting Hephaestus drunk and bringing him to Mount Olympus carried on top of a mule.

DIONYSUS

Hephaestus and His Bride, Aphrodite

Once Hephaestus regained his senses, he agreed to release his mother, but some stories say that Zeus offered him the beautiful Aphrodite as his wife. Zeus did this because Aphrodite needed to be kept away from the other gods. Her beauty was so overwhelming that many gods and mortal men wanted to be with her. Hephaestus was happy with this offer of Aphrodite's hand in marriage so he released his mother from her golden chair.

However, Aphrodite was very displeased. She was in love with Ares, the god of war, and wanted nothing to do with this ugly, crippled metalworker. She was stuck marrying him, but had no intention of changing her flirtatious ways.

ARES

HELIOS

APHRODITE IS UNFAITHFUL TO HER HUSBAND

All the other gods and goddesses knew that soon after her marriage, Aphrodite began to see Ares in secret. For a long time, Hephaestus didn't suspect his lovely wife. The romantic meetings between Aphrodite and Ares continued and finally Helios, the god of the sun, could no longer stay silent on the matter. He pulled Hephaestus aside and told him about his wife's unfaithfulness.

The Golden Net

Hephaestus created a strong golden net that couldn't be broken. It was his plan to ensnare Aphrodite and Ares. He told Aphrodite that he would be gone for a few days. Of course, he planned to come back at an inappropriate time. He caught Ares and Aphrodite as they were in a romantic embrace. He threw the net over them and dragged them both to Mount Olympus so that everyone would see the evidence of Aphrodite's unfaithfulness.

NET

When they got to Mount Olympus, Hephaestus expected that the gods and goddesses would punish Ares and Aphrodite, but instead they laughed because the two had been caught. Ares agreed to make a payment of a fine for his crime. Aphrodite became pregnant and eventually gave birth to Harmonia, who was also a goddess. Some of the Greek myths say that after this happened Hephaestus and Aphrodite divorced each other.

This wasn't the end of the revenge part of the story. In his fiery rage over what had happened, Hephaestus created a necklace, which was called the necklace of Harmonia. It was cursed and everyone who possessed it, suffered great tragedy.

ANCIENT TEMPLE IN THEBES

HARMONIA'S NECKLACE

When Harmonia was of marrying age, she was engaged to Cadmus, who was the founder of the Greek city of Thebes. When Hephaetus found out about the impending marriage, he offered her a beautiful necklace. It was crafted with gold and abundant jewels and it had two entwined serpents with their mouths open to create a clasp. Little did Harmonia know that Hephaestus had put a magical curse on this wedding gift.

Eventually Harmonia and her husband were turned into serpents and their daughter, a mortal woman who was named Semele, inherited the wicked object. The day that Semele wore it she died. On that day, Hera came to her in disguise. Semele was in a romantic involvement with Hera's husband Zeus.

SERPENT

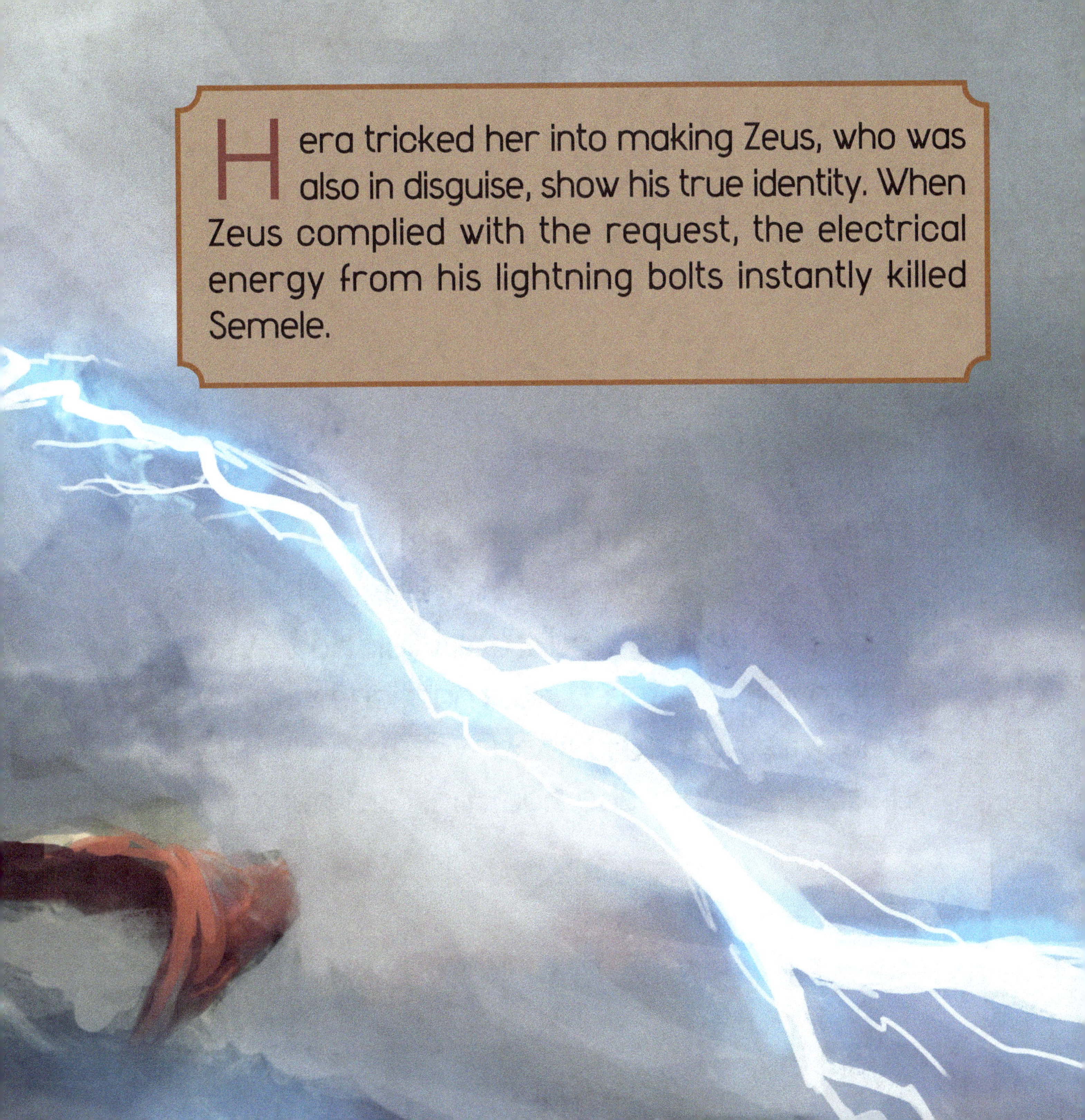

Hera tricked her into making Zeus, who was also in disguise, show his true identity. When Zeus complied with the request, the electrical energy from his lightning bolts instantly killed Semele.

The next person to be subjected to tragedy was Queen Jocasta. The necklace of Harmonia kept her young and beautiful. However, she unknowingly entered into marriage with her son, who was named Oedipus. Eventually, Jocasta discovered that she had married her own son.

QUEEN JOCASTA

OEDIPUS WITH DAUGHTER ANTIGON

She killed herself and Oedipus gouged his own eyes out. The chain of tragedy continued and the necklace passed through many more hands causing immense suffering to all who touched it.

SUMMARY

The Greek myths weren't always consistent in their storylines. A famous story about Hephaestus, the god of fire and blacksmithing, was that Hera gave birth to him by herself and that he was lame and ugly at birth. Hera rejected him and threw him off Mount Olympus. When he discovered his mother's rejection, he crafted a golden chair from which she couldn't emerge.

Zeus bribed him by offering the goddess of love, Aphrodite, as his bride. Aphrodite didn't want to marry Hephaestus because he was ugly and lame. She was unfaithful to him with Ares the god of war, but Hephaestus caught them in their crime and threw an unbreakable golden net over them.

Awesome! Now that you've read about the marriage of Aphrodite and Hephaestus you may want to read another story from Greek mythology in the Baby Professor book Dionysus: Killed Many Times, Survived Every Time – Greek Mythology for Kids   Children's Greek & Roman Books.

www.ingramcontent.com/pod-product-compliance
Lightning Source LLC
Chambersburg PA
CBHW060227120726

48009CB00003B/171